S0-AXW-027

Niles Public Library District
6960 Oakton Street • Niles, Illinois 60714
Phone 847-663-1234

DATE DUE	DATE DUE

OCT   2000

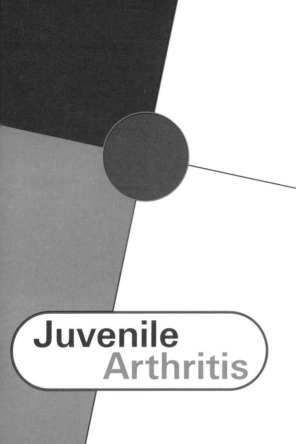

Juvenile Arthritis

By Judith Peacock

Consultant:
Barbara E. Ostrov, MD
Associate Professor of Pediatrics and Medicine
Adult Rheumatology and Pediatric Rheumatology
PennState Geisinger Health System
Hershey Medical Center

Perspectives on Disease and Illness

LifeMatters
an imprint of Capstone Press
Mankato, Minnesota

LifeMatters books are published by Capstone Press
818 North Willow Street • Mankato, Minnesota 56001
http://www.capstone-press.com

©2000 Capstone Press. All rights reserved. No part of this book may be reproduced or transmitted in any form or by any means without written permission from the publisher. The publisher takes no responsibility for the use of any of the materials or methods described in this book nor for the products thereof.

Printed in the United States of America

Library of Congress Cataloging-in-Publication Data
Peacock, Judith, 1942–
      Juvenile arthritis/by Judith Peacock
            p. cm. — (Perspectives on disease and illness)
      Includes bibliographical references and index.
      Summary: Discusses the types of arthritis, the treatment and complications of juvenile rheumatoid arthritis, and research related to this disease.
      ISBN 0-7368-0279-7. — ISBN 0-7368-0294-0
      1. Rheumatoid arthritis in children Juvenile literature.
      2. Rheumatoid arthritis in children—Research Juvenile literature.
      [1. Rheumatoid arthritis. 2. Diseases.] I. Title. II. Series.
      RJ482.A77P43 2000
      618.92´7227—dc 21   99-23863
                           CIP

Staff Credits
Kristin Thoennes, editor; Adam Lazar, designer; Kimberly Danger, photo researcher

Photo Credits
Cover: The Stock Market/©Pete Saloutos, bottom; PNI/©Digital Vision, left, right; PNI/©Rubberball, middle
©Index Stock Photography, Inc./47
International Stock/©Don Romero, 51; ©Bob Jacobson, 10; ©Michael Agliolo, 7; ©Bill Tucker, 28; ©Stan Pak, 35
Photri Inc./49
Rainbow/©Linda K. Moore, 32
©James L. Shaffer, 9, 41
Tom Stack & Assoc./David M. Dennis, 16, 58; ©Tom & Therisa Stack, 45
Transparencies/©Tom McCarthy, 25; ©Michael Moore, 22, 31
Unicorn Stock Photos/©D & I MacDonald, 18; ©Jeff Greenberg, 38, 56; ©Tom McCarthy, 55

A 0 9 8 7 6 5 4 3 2 1

Table of Contents

Chapter Overview

People with arthritis have something wrong with their joints. Juvenile rheumatoid arthritis is the most common form of arthritis among children age 16 and younger.

Inflammation of the joints is the most common symptom, or sign, of juvenile rheumatoid arthritis. The joints are swollen and stiff. Pain and redness sometimes occur as well.

Sometimes children and teens with juvenile rheumatoid arthritis have difficulty moving the affected joints. It can hurt to do even the simplest task.

Juvenile rheumatoid arthritis affects individuals differently. The effects range from mild to severe. Some children and teens outgrow juvenile rheumatoid arthritis. Others have arthritis the rest of their life.

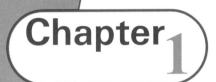

Chapter 1

What Is Arthritis?

Hannah's albarm clock went off at 5:00 A.M. Hannah, Age 13
Hannah groaned. Every joint and muscle in her body ached. It was going to be a bad day.

Hannah struggled to move. Her arms and legs felt as stiff as boards. After awhile, she finally managed to pull herself out of bed.

Hannah soaked in a tub of warm water. She began to feel a little better. Then she got dressed slowly. It still hurt to move. She had a hard time lifting her arm to comb her hair. Hannah sighed. It would be a bad hair day, too.

Hannah has arthritis. When her arthritis acts up, she needs a lot of time to get going in the morning.

You can get arthritis in your neck, jaw, shoulders, elbows, wrists, hands, fingers, hips, back, knees, ankles, feet, and toes.

Not an Old Folks' Disease

Some people picture gray-haired grandparents when they hear the word *arthritis*. The fact is that children and teens get arthritis, too.

There are over 100 different types of arthritis. Any of these types can develop in children and teens. When arthritis develops before the age of 16, it is called juvenile arthritis. The most common form of arthritis among young people is juvenile rheumatoid arthritis. This book focuses on that form of arthritis.

A Disease of the Joints

Arthritis affects the joints. A joint is a place where two bones come together. Joints are like hinges on a door. They allow people to move. Joints make walking, running, skateboarding, dancing, and many other activities possible.

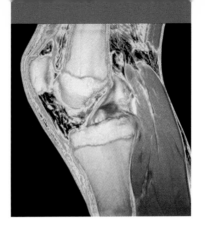

Joints have several parts. Cartilage covers the end of each bone. This soft tissue keeps bones from rubbing together. A capsule, or sac, encloses the entire joint.

A tissue called synovium lines the capsule. The synovium releases a fluid. Synovial fluid acts like motor oil in a car engine. It allows the parts of the joint to move freely so they do not rub against one another.

The word *arthritis* means "inflammation of the joints." *Inflammation* usually means "swelling." Many types of arthritis do involve swelling of the joints. Other types, however, do not involve swelling.

What Is Juvenile Rheumatoid Arthritis?

Inflammation of the joints is the main symptom, or sign, of juvenile rheumatoid arthritis. The synovium produces too much synovial fluid. The excess fluid stretches the joint capsule. The joint becomes swollen and stiff.

Myth: A cold, damp climate can cause arthritis.

Fact: A cold, damp climate does not cause arthritis. It can, however, make arthritis pain feel worse.

What Causes Juvenile Rheumatoid Arthritis?

The body's immune system plays a role in causing juvenile rheumatoid arthritis. The immune system normally protects the body against illness. White blood cells attack invading viruses and bacteria. Viruses and bacteria are types of germs. For some unknown reason, in people with rheumatoid arthritis, the white blood cells multiply and turn on the body. They attack the lining of the joints. The result is swelling and inflammation.

Who Gets Juvenile Rheumatoid Arthritis?

A child as young as six months or younger can have juvenile rheumatoid arthritis. The disease also may develop during the teen years. Juvenile rheumatoid arthritis is not contagious. It cannot be passed from person to person like a cold or the flu.

What Is Juvenile Rheumatoid Arthritis Like?

Juvenile rheumatoid arthritis affects joints in several ways. The arthritis makes an affected joint difficult to move. Children with arthritis may have trouble eating, dressing, writing, or doing other daily activities. They may have trouble walking.

It also hurts to move the affected joint. As a result, children with arthritis may avoid using the joint. The joint may become bent in a fixed position. This is called a contracture. Muscles that support a joint may become weak from lack of use. Severe arthritis that lasts a long time can permanently damage a joint.

Juvenile rheumatoid arthritis was diagnosed in Raymond when he was four years old. Medications and other forms of treatment could not stop the inflammation. The inflammation permanently distorted his joints. His fingers are now bent like claws. His left foot bends out at an angle. Raymond must use crutches or a wheelchair to get around.

Raymond, Age 17

Flares

Juvenile rheumatoid arthritis is unpredictable. It comes and goes without warning. Sometimes the disease is active. This is called a flare. Sometimes the disease seems to go away for a long time. Many years may pass without any symptoms. This is called a remission.

A child or teen with juvenile rheumatoid arthritis may go several weeks or months between flares. Symptoms of the disease can change from day to day. They may be mild one day and severe the next. Symptoms can even change from morning to afternoon. This unpredictability makes juvenile rheumatoid arthritis even more difficult to live with.

Fast Fact

Each year, about 50,000 youngsters are diagnosed with juvenile rheumatoid arthritis.

Patty has arthritis in her right knee. This doesn't stop her from dancing. Patty tried out for her high-school musical. She got the part of a dancer in the chorus. Sure enough, on opening night she had a flare. Her knee was swollen and painful. Patty had to watch the performance from backstage.

Patty, Age 16

The Long-Term Outlook

Juvenile rheumatoid arthritis affects each person differently. Some children and teens may have one or two bouts of the disease. Then the arthritis disappears forever. For other young people, the disease continues into their adult years. It becomes a chronic condition. This means that it lasts for a long time.

Some children and teens have only a mild form of the disease. Most of the time, however, they can be as active as other young people. In severe cases, the disease can cause deformities and crippling. It can stunt growth. Even if someone outgrows the disease, he or she may have damaged joints.

George F. Still, a British doctor, first identified juvenile rheumatoid arthritis in 1897. Until recently, doctors thought juvenile rheumatoid arthritis and adult rheumatoid arthritis were the same disease. Inflammation of the joints is common to both. Differences are now being discovered. For example, total remission occurs much more often in juvenile rheumatoid arthritis. Most adults with rheumatoid arthritis have joint inflammation all of their life.

Fast
Fast

Points to Consider

How do you think people with arthritis feel about remission?

Do any of your family members have arthritis? What is the disease like for them?

Do any teens in your school have juvenile rheumatoid arthritis? What is the disease like for them?

Chapter Overview

There are three main types of juvenile rheumatoid arthritis.

Pauciarticular juvenile rheumatoid arthritis affects four or fewer joints. It often affects just one joint, usually the knee. There are two types of pauciarticular juvenile rheumatoid arthritis.

Polyarticular juvenile rheumatoid arthritis affects five or more joints. It usually affects the same joints on both sides of the body. Children with this type may be small and thin for their age.

Systemic juvenile rheumatoid arthritis affects the internal organs as well as the joints. It is the most serious form. A high fever and pink rash accompany flares.

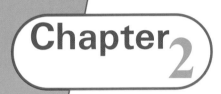

Chapter 2

Types of Juvenile Rheumatoid Arthritis

There are three main types of juvenile rheumatoid arthritis. The type depends on the number of joints affected. The specific joints affected also determine the type. Inflammation of the joints is common to all types.

Pauciarticular Juvenile Rheumatoid Arthritis

Pauciarticular juvenile rheumatoid arthritis affects four or fewer joints. *Pauci-* means "few." Most often, this type of arthritis involves only one or two joints. Usually these are the large joints such as the knees, elbows, and ankles. This type usually affects the joints on just one side of the body. For example, a child may have arthritis in the left knee but not the right. Pauciarticular juvenile rheumatoid arthritis is sometimes called oligoarticular arthritis.

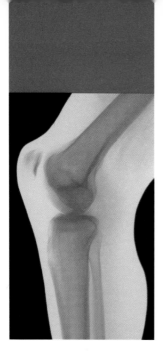

There are two types of pauciarticular juvenile rheumatoid arthritis. In the most common type, pauci I, the arthritis often begins before age five. More girls than boys get this type. The average age of onset is three years.

Children with this type of pauciarticular juvenile rheumatoid arthritis are at risk of a silent eye disease. They should have their eyes checked regularly. The eye can become inflamed with no symptoms. This can lead to serious vision problems if untreated.

The second type of pauciarticular juvenile rheumatoid arthritis, pauci II, affects older children and usually boys. The average age of onset is eight years. The eyes are usually not affected with this type.

The legs and spine are affected in pauci II. Usually they are inflamed. If the arthritis affects one leg, the child's two legs may grow at different rates. The child may walk with a limp. This is true for both types of pauciarticular juvenile rheumatoid arthritis.

Juvenile Arthritis

You can get an idea of what it's like to have arthritis in your hands. Tape your thumb to your palm. Then try turning on a lamp, tying your shoelaces, or writing your name.

Polyarticular Juvenile Rheumatoid Arthritis

Polyarticular juvenile rheumatoid arthritis affects five or more joints. *Poly-* means "many." This type of arthritis usually affects the small joints of the fingers and hands. It also can affect the knees, hips, ankles, feet, neck, and jaw. This type often affects the same joints on both sides of the body.

Debbie has polyarticular juvenile rheumatoid arthritis in her hands and feet. It is often hard for her to grasp things. Her toothbrush and hairbrush have very thick handles. She can wrap her hands around those special handles more easily.

Debbie, Age 14

Girls are twice as likely to get polyarticular juvenile rheumatoid arthritis as boys. It often starts during the teen years. It can cause more pain and stiffness than pauciarticular juvenile rheumatoid arthritis. Children with this type may be small and thin for their age. They may also have anemia. Anemia is a problem with too little iron in the red blood cells. Anemia can make a person feel tired all the time.

Systemic Juvenile Rheumatoid Arthritis

Paul was reading one Saturday afternoon when he began to feel sick. His temperature was 102.6. Later that day, he noticed a rash on his body. Paul's stomach hurt, and he had chest pains.

Paul, Age 16

Paul has systemic juvenile rheumatoid arthritis. Systemic refers to the whole body. This is the least common form of juvenile rheumatoid arthritis. It is also the most serious form. Some doctors refer to it as Still's disease.

Systemic juvenile rheumatoid arthritis affects the internal organs as well as the joints. There may be inflammation around the heart. The liver and spleen can become enlarged.

Systemic juvenile rheumatoid arthritis usually comes on suddenly. The person may have a high fever for a few hours. Then the person's temperature returns to normal. The high fever may return a short time later. A pink rash is another symptom of this type of juvenile rheumatoid arthritis.

Here are other types of juvenile arthritis:

- *Psoriatic arthritis* (arthritis plus scaly, red rash on scalp or near joints)
- *Arthritis of inflammatory bowel disease* (arthritis plus inflamed intestines)
- *Reiter's syndrome* (inflammation in joints, urinary tract, and eyes)
- *Ankylosing spondylitis* (arthritis that mainly affects spine and hips)

Systemic juvenile rheumatoid arthritis affects males and females equally. It can begin during childhood or during the teen years. The systemic features may disappear. About half of the people who have it, however, continue to have stiffness and pain in the joints.

Points to Consider

How might juvenile rheumatoid arthritis affect a teen's growth?

What activities of daily living might be difficult for a person with juvenile rheumatoid arthritis?

Teens with juvenile rheumatoid arthritis often feel like they have a bad case of flu during a flare. Describe how you feel when you have the flu.

Have you ever felt stiff and sore from too much exercise? How did you relieve the pain?

Chapter Overview

Diagnosing juvenile rheumatoid arthritis can be difficult. Many illnesses as well as broken bones can cause joint pain.

Doctors go through several steps to diagnose juvenile rheumatoid arthritis. They gather information about the person's background and conduct a physical examination. They also order laboratory tests to rule out other diseases.

Doctors follow certain guidelines to reach a diagnosis of juvenile rheumatoid arthritis. These include how long the pain has lasted and the person's age when the pain began.

Chapter 3

Diagnosing Juvenile Rheumatoid Arthritis

Symptoms of Juvenile Rheumatoid Arthritis

Tessa is a teen with polyarticular juvenile rheumatoid arthritis. She was diagnosed when  she was 12 years old. Her mother noticed that Tessa was cranky, especially in the morning. When Tessa and her mother went shopping, Tessa complained about being tired. She wanted to sit down frequently. Tessa began having trouble sleeping at night. She said her sore legs kept her awake. Soon Tessa was complaining of pain in her knees and elbows.

Tessa's symptoms puzzled her doctor. He could find no infection or other illness. Tessa's mother took Tessa to see a doctor who specializes in cancer. That doctor ruled out cancer. Finally, they went to see a doctor who specializes in inflammatory arthritis. The rheumatologist suspected that Tessa might have juvenile rheumatoid arthritis. This eventually proved to be the case.

Diagnosing juvenile rheumatoid arthritis can be difficult. Many diseases cause joint pain. Also, there is no single test for juvenile rheumatoid arthritis. Diagnosing it is a matter of ruling out other causes.

Joint pain is the main symptom of juvenile rheumatoid arthritis. The joints appear swollen. They may feel warm from the outside. Other symptoms of juvenile rheumatoid arthritis include:

Morning stiffness
Fatigue
Loss of appetite
Weight loss
Fever
Night sweats

Steps in Diagnosing Juvenile Rheumatoid Arthritis

Doctors go through several steps before diagnosing juvenile rheumatoid arthritis. First, they ask about the person's symptoms. They want to know when the stiffness began, how long it usually lasts, and which joints are affected. They also ask about the person's medical history. They want to know about past medical problems and whether anyone in the family has had arthritis. Some types of arthritis run in families, but usually not juvenile rheumatoid arthritis.

Did You Know?

Growing pains are deep, cramping pains in the thigh, shin, or calf. They usually happen in the evening or during the night. The cause of growing pains is unknown. They are not a form of arthritis.

The next step is to examine the person. Doctors look for inflamed joints and rashes. They also look for lumps under the skin. An eye examination is another important part of diagnosis.

Laboratory tests are an important step in diagnosis. Doctors order tests of the blood and urine. These tests help to determine if other diseases might be causing the person's problems. Doctors might order tests of fluids from the person's joints. X rays can reveal if a bone infection, tumor, or fracture is causing the joint pain. A fracture is a break or crack.

Doctors use all this information to help them work toward a diagnosis of juvenile rheumatoid arthritis. In addition, they see if the following points are true:

The arthritis is in the same joint or joints at least six weeks in a row.

The symptoms begin before age 16.

All other causes have been eliminated.

Here are conditions in which arthritis may be present:

- Juvenile systemic lupus erythematosus (inflammation in organs)
- Dermatomyositis (inflamed skin and muscle tissue)
- Scleroderma (thickened skin)
- Vasculitis (inflamed blood vessels)

After the Diagnosis

A diagnosis of juvenile rheumatoid arthritis is a relief to some people. They are glad to finally know the cause of the pain. They also are glad that the disease is not fatal. Other people react with shock and anger. A diagnosis of juvenile rheumatoid arthritis can be especially difficult for active teens. They no longer may be able to do the things they are used to doing.

Brian, Age 15

Brian's right knee kept swelling up. His doctor diagnosed pauciarticular juvenile rheumatoid arthritis. Brian became very upset. He believed he would never play first base again. Brian pretended he didn't have juvenile rheumatoid arthritis. Then his coach said Brian could permanently damage his knee. The coach convinced Brian to seek treatment.

Brian's physical therapist showed him special exercises to train for baseball. The therapist also put together some padding to protect Brian's knee. When Brian has a flare, the coach sends in a pinch runner.

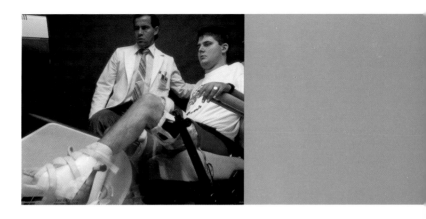

In some people, juvenile rheumatoid arthritis can go into remission. In others, it cannot be cured, but it can be controlled. It is important to begin treatment before joints become permanently damaged.

Points to Consider

Do you know anyone who has symptoms of juvenile rheumatoid arthritis? How does the person cope with the disease?

How would having juvenile rheumatoid arthritis change your life?

Have you ever had something wrong with you but didn't know the reason? How did you feel?

Chapter Overview

There is no cure for juvenile rheumatoid arthritis or other forms of arthritis. Treatment might make people feel better and move better. It also might prevent joint damage. Occasionally people can go into remission with help from medication.

Medications and exercise are important treatments for juvenile rheumatoid arthritis. Other treatments include wearing splints, applying heat, and eating properly. Splints help keep body parts straight. Surgery is sometimes performed to correct problems or replace joints.

Teens with juvenile rheumatoid arthritis need to beware of fake cures. Managing pain takes hard work.

Chapter 4

Controlling Juvenile Rheumatoid Arthritis

Treatment for juvenile rheumatoid arthritis has three main goals. One goal is to control inflammation and relieve pain. The second goal is to prevent or control joint damage. The third goal is to increase the body's ability to move.

Medications

Medications are the main treatment for juvenile rheumatoid arthritis. Doctors prescribe drugs based on the type of juvenile rheumatoid arthritis. Drugs affect people in different ways. A person may try several drugs before finding one that helps.

Medications for juvenile rheumatoid arthritis vary in strength. Doctors worry about side effects in growing children and teens. Doctors try to treat the arthritis with weaker drugs first.

Anti-inflammatory drugs such as aspirin or ibuprofen often are used in treating juvenile rheumatoid arthritis. These medicines can irritate the stomach. They must be taken with food. A person with the flu or chicken pox must not take aspirin. Doctors must closely monitor the use of aspirin.

If necessary, doctors may prescribe prednisone or cortisone for severe cases. In higher dosages, these drugs can cause rapid weight gain and bone loss. Antirheumatic drugs can slow or quiet down arthritis in many people.

Medications for juvenile rheumatoid arthritis come in capsule, tablet, or liquid form. Some may be injected directly into a muscle, a vein, or the joint itself. All medications should be watched closely for side effects. Very strong drugs may need to be given in a doctor's office. Then the doctor can monitor the drug's effects on the person.

Your pet dog or cat can have osteoarthritis. The joints in older animals can begin to break down. Treatment to relieve pain is the same as for humans.

Tracy and her doctor tried several drugs to manage Tracy's arthritis. They finally found the right combination. Tracy takes one antirheumatic tablet every day. She also takes aspirin as needed for pain.

Tracy, Age 18

At first, Tracy went to the doctor's office once a week for a shot. The lab tested her blood before she could get the shot. After six months, Tracy was able to take pills at home. The pills seem to work. Tracy has fewer flares. She feels better, and she moves better.

Exercise

Exercise is an important part of treatment for juvenile rheumatoid arthritis. Joints must be moved. Otherwise, muscles become weak. Exercise is the only thing that can keep joints moving fully. Drugs cannot do this.

Therapeutic exercise helps people regain or improve movement. One kind of therapeutic exercise is called range of motion. These stretching exercises make joints more flexible. There are different range-of-motion exercises for different parts of the body. Strengthening exercises are another kind of therapeutic exercise. They help to build muscle. These exercises must be done every day.

Smoking is hazardous to everyone's health. It may be especially dangerous for those with juvenile rheumatoid arthritis. Recent studies indicate that smoking makes the symptoms of rheumatoid arthritis worse. Smoking also increases the risk of stomach complications from anti-inflammatory drugs.

Sports and recreational activities are a good way to exercise joints and muscles. Children and teens with juvenile rheumatoid arthritis also can relax and have fun with their friends. Swimming is one of the best forms of exercise for people with juvenile rheumatoid arthritis. They don't have to bear weight on painful joints. Contact sports such as football generally are not recommended. Doctors can advise people on safe ways to participate in most sports.

Splints

Splints are another form of treatment. These devices keep joints in the correct position and help relieve pain. A joint may be fixed in a contracture. A splint can help stretch the joint back to a normal position.

People usually wear splints at night. These are called resting splints. Sometimes people wear splints during the day to make daily activities easier. These are called active, or functional, splints. Splints are custom made for each person. They must be adjusted as a child or teen grows or as joint positions change.

Diet

Juvenile rheumatoid arthritis often leads to problems with weight. Children and teens may lose weight if they feel too tired to eat. Opening and closing the mouth may be painful. Side effects from drugs may upset the stomach. Some drugs cause children to gain weight. Children and teens also may gain weight if they fail to exercise. Too much weight puts extra stress on joints.

Surgery

Surgery may be performed in the later stages of juvenile rheumatoid arthritis. One type of surgery replaces damaged joints with artificial joints. Hip and knee replacements are the most common. Another type of surgery repairs contractures. Surgeons cut the tight tissues. This allows the joint to return to a normal position.

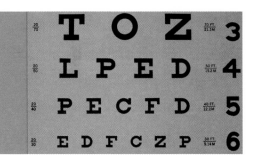

Other Important Parts of Treatment

Treatment for juvenile rheumatoid arthritis includes several other important parts.

Occupational therapy

Occupational therapy helps people learn to do daily activities. For example, teens with juvenile rheumatoid arthritis may have difficulty lifting their legs or bending over. Putting on or taking off a pair of shoes can be painful. An occupational therapist can show teens how to use a special shoehorn to make the task easier.

Heat

A warm bath, heated swimming pool, or electric heating pad helps relieve pain. Heat feels soothing. Warm water can help stiff joints feel looser.

Dental care

Teens with juvenile rheumatoid arthritis may have difficulty brushing and flossing their teeth. Medications can damage teeth and gums. Regular checkups and professional cleanings are important.

Eye care

Teens at risk for eye problems should have an eye exam at least every six months. An ophthalmologist should conduct the exam. These eye doctors make sure the teen's eyes are healthy.

Rest

Juvenile rheumatoid arthritis can cause extreme fatigue.
Medications can make teens feel tired, too. It is important to get
enough rest.

Stress management

Feeling tense and worried can add to a teen's pain. Books, tapes,
and special classes are available to help teens cope with stress.

False Treatments

Abby has severe systemic juvenile
rheumatoid arthritis. She saw an ad in the
back of a magazine. The ad was for a miracle cure for arthritis.
Abby sent $39.95 to the address in the ad. Then she waited and
waited for the miracle cure to arrive.

Abby, Age 15

Finally, a package came. A small tube of ointment was inside.
Abby followed the directions on the tube. She spread the
ointment on her swollen joints every day. Soon the tube was
empty. Abby still had pain. She was very disappointed. She
also was mad that she had wasted her money.

Here are some recent quack cures for arthritis:

- Wear a copper bracelet
- Sit in an abandoned uranium mine
- Eat seaweed
- Take iodine
- Drink "immunized" milk
- Have your teeth pulled
- Wear special underwear

Abby was a victim of quackery. Quack cures promise quick, easy solutions to difficult problems. There is no scientific proof that they work. Quackery often targets people with arthritis. They may be tempted to believe these false claims because they want to end their pain.

Quackery can be dangerous. It can keep people from getting beneficial treatment from a doctor. Some quack cures can make people feel worse. Fad diets, drugs, and devices may even lead to serious medical problems.

Teens with juvenile rheumatoid arthritis can learn to recognize quack cures. First, there is no cure for arthritis at the present time. If there were, it would be in the headlines of all the newspapers. It would not be advertised in the back of a magazine. Second, if something sounds too good to be true, it probably is.

Points to Consider

Why might it be hard for a teen with juvenile rheumatoid arthritis to stick with a treatment plan?

How could you help a friend with juvenile rheumatoid arthritis follow his or her treatment plan?

Have you seen ads for health and beauty aids that seemed too good to be true? Describe them.

Chapter Overview

School presents special challenges to students with juvenile rheumatoid arthritis. They may have difficulty keeping up with schoolwork. They may struggle getting to school or around the building.

There are solutions to most of the difficulties students with juvenile rheumatoid arthritis face. Teachers, parents, and students can work together to make sure the students get a good education.

Students with juvenile rheumatoid arthritis may have to educate teachers and other students about their disease. Some teachers and students may not understand their illness.

Chapter 5

Surviving School

Keeping Up

Students with juvenile rheumatoid arthritis may have a hard time keeping up with their schoolwork. They may miss classes because of frequent visits to the doctor. On some days they may feel too ill to go to school.

Teachers expect students to take notes in class and write papers and tests. These tasks can be extremely difficult for a student whose hands are stiff with arthritis. Juvenile rheumatoid arthritis can cause fatigue. Students with juvenile rheumatoid arthritis may lack the energy to complete assignments.

There are ways for students with juvenile rheumatoid arthritis to keep up with their schoolwork. They can:

Find out which day or time of day is best to be gone from school.

Pick someone in each class to tell them about missed assignments.

Tape-record lectures and class discussions. Ask a classmate to take notes.

Answer test questions orally or tape-record test answers.

Ask the teacher for more time to complete assignments.

Getting Around

High school students must go from class to class. They usually have only a few minutes to do this. They may have to go from one end of the building to another or up and down stairs. They must carry books and other supplies with them. Teens with juvenile rheumatoid arthritis may have difficulty getting around the school building.

Regular communication between home and school is important in helping a student with juvenile rheumatoid arthritis. At the beginning of the year, students might give their teachers a packet of information about juvenile rheumatoid arthritis. Teachers, parents, and teens might meet to talk about the young person's needs.

Tonya, Age 17

Tonya uses crutches because of her juvenile rheumatoid arthritis. Her teachers allow her to leave class early. This gives her extra time to get to the next class. She also avoids the crowded hallways. Tonya has two copies of each textbook. She keeps one in the classroom and one at home. This way she doesn't have to carry books with her. Tonya carries pencils, paper, and pens in a fanny pack.

Relating to Others

Many people do not know about juvenile rheumatoid arthritis. This may cause problems for students with the disease. Some teachers may become impatient or angry. They may view the student's inability to keep up as laziness or carelessness. This is especially true if the student has no visible signs of the disease.

Grant, Age 15

At the beginning of the school year, Grant writes a letter to each of his teachers. He explains about juvenile rheumatoid arthritis. He tells them what he can and cannot do. Grant asks his teachers to treat him like any other student. He doesn't want them to go easy on him just because he has juvenile rheumatoid arthritis.

Surviving School

At a
Glance

In the United States, these laws guarantee the educational rights of disabled students:
- Rehabilitation Act of 1973
- Individuals With Disabilities Education Act, 1990
- Americans With Disabilities Act, 1990

In Canada, the Charter of Rights and Freedoms protects people with disabilities. It is part of the Constitution Act of 1982.

Some students may make fun of a teen with juvenile rheumatoid arthritis. This is especially true if the teen has a limp or uses crutches or a wheelchair. Other students may be curious about juvenile rheumatoid arthritis. They may wonder why the teen wears wrist splints or uses a footrest.

Joe has used a wheelchair for the last five years. He tries to be active in his school and community. He shares the facts about juvenile rheumatoid arthritis whenever he can. Joe finds that the more people get to know him, the more they accept him.

Joe, Age 17

Working Together

Teachers, parents, and students can work together to help students with juvenile rheumatoid arthritis get a good education. In the United States, public schools must guarantee disabled students an education appropriate to their needs. It is the law. A student with juvenile rheumatoid arthritis may not be able to walk to the school bus stop. In this case, the school might send a special bus or van to the student's home.

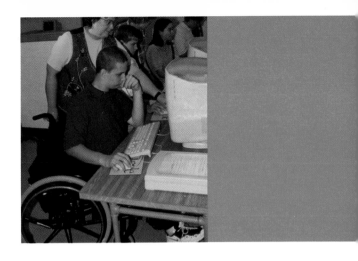

Most schools now have wheelchair ramps and elevators to help disabled students get around. A student with juvenile rheumatoid arthritis might get too stiff sitting at a regular desk. In this case, the school might provide a special posture chair and desktop.

The school might modify some classes to meet the needs of a student with juvenile rheumatoid arthritis. Many students with juvenile rheumatoid arthritis need an adapted physical education class. School officials need to be aware of this need. Otherwise the student could be hurt from trying to participate in activities that aren't good for his or her body.

Points to Consider

What does your school do to help people with physical disabilities move around?

How could you help a teen with juvenile rheumatoid arthritis in the classroom? in the hallway? in the lunchroom? in the bathroom? in the locker room?

Your classmates are teasing a student with juvenile rheumatoid arthritis. What would you do?

Chapter Overview

Juvenile rheumatoid arthritis can make activities of daily living more difficult.

Juvenile rheumatoid arthritis can affect a teen's self-esteem and ability to fit in. Teens with juvenile rheumatoid arthritis wonder who should know about their disease. They wonder if they will be able to have friends and date. Juvenile rheumatoid arthritis may make it difficult to get along with family members.

Teens with juvenile rheumatoid arthritis can learn to cope with their special problems. They do not need to feel alone. Many people are available to help.

Chapter 6

Living With Juvenile Rheumatoid Arthritis

Most teens with juvenile rheumatoid arthritis are able to manage daily activities. They learn to adapt. They plan more time for dressing and eating. They use special devices. Teens with juvenile rheumatoid arthritis also must deal with special concerns and feelings. These may not be as easy to manage.

Fast
Fact

Juvenile rheumatoid arthritis is the second leading cause of chronic illness in children 16 and younger. Asthma is number one.

Maintaining Self-Esteem

Juvenile rheumatoid arthritis can affect how teens feel about themselves. Teens with the disease may have poor self-esteem. For one thing, juvenile rheumatoid arthritis can make a teen self-conscious about appearance. The teen might have a limp, hand deformity, or rash. Side effects of medications can influence a person's appearance. Prednisone or cortisone, for example, can cause a person to look bloated or puffy.

Teens with juvenile rheumatoid arthritis may feel bad about themselves because they are unable to do certain things. They may not be able to walk as quickly as other people. They may not be able to participate in sports. Most teens with juvenile rheumatoid arthritis want to be independent. It can be hard to ask other people to open doors or lift things.

Doug wears braces on his legs because of his juvenile rheumatoid arthritis. He knows **Doug, Age 12** he will never be a track star. Doug focuses on developing his creative and mental abilities instead. He learned a lot about computers. Other kids think he's a computer whiz. They come to him for help with their computer problems.

Fitting In

Most teens want to be like other teens. Juvenile rheumatoid arthritis makes it difficult to fit in. Ongoing pain may keep teens with this disease from doing the things others do. Teens like to stay out late. Those with juvenile rheumatoid arthritis may need to stay home and rest. Teens move fast and are always on the go. Those with the disease may need a lot of time to get going.

Teens with juvenile rheumatoid arthritis need to take medicine, go to physical therapy, and visit the doctor frequently. This makes them different from most other teens. This disease can interfere with a teenage lifestyle.

Teens with juvenile rheumatoid arthritis are able to get their driver's license. However, they may not be able to drive during a flare. Some teens with juvenile rheumatoid arthritis may need a car with special controls.

Telling Others

Teens with juvenile rheumatoid arthritis wonder what they should tell others about their disease. They want other people to understand. They don't want other people to feel sorry for them. They don't want special treatment. Teens with juvenile rheumatoid arthritis may wonder what to tell a date. This problem often solves itself. The right time to explain usually comes naturally.

When Carrie began dating, she worried a lot. She worried about getting stiff in the middle of a movie. She worried about not being able to put her arms around her boyfriend. Carrie decided it was best to be honest from the start. Then she wouldn't find herself in an uncomfortable situation.

Carrie, Age 16

Teens with juvenile rheumatoid arthritis should tell a few close friends. Good friends want to know how they can support each other.

Dealing With Families

Juvenile rheumatoid arthritis can cause stress in a family. It takes more time to care for a child with juvenile rheumatoid arthritis. Parents may worry about doctor bills and the high cost of medications. They might want to overprotect their child. They may not let him or her do things other teens do. They might excuse the teen from doing chores around the house. Brothers and sisters may resent the attention their sibling receives.

Teens with juvenile rheumatoid arthritis need the love and support of their family. Teens need help to manage their illness. Most families find that talking openly and honestly helps ease problems. They also find that it works best to give the teen with juvenile rheumatoid arthritis a life that is as normal as possible. Juvenile rheumatoid arthritis can have a positive effect on the family. The whole family can exercise and eat a healthy diet along with the teen with juvenile rheumatoid arthritis.

Arthritis is sometimes called the hidden disease. Others cannot always see the stiffness and swelling. Other people may not believe the person with arthritis is in pain.

Coping With Juvenile Rheumatoid Arthritis

Teens with juvenile rheumatoid arthritis not only can survive their illness but also can thrive with it. If you are a teen with juvenile rheumatoid arthritis, you can do these things to cope:

Form a team of health care professionals.

If possible, your team should include a pediatric rheumatologist. Other members might be a physical therapist, an occupational therapist, an eye doctor, a dietitian, and a mental health counselor. Choose team members with whom you feel comfortable. Share decision making about your health.

Follow your treatment plan.

Take your medications as prescribed. Exercise regularly. You will feel better. You also will help minimize damage to your joints and improve your muscle strength. If you have a problem with your treatment plan, talk with your health care team.

Pay attention to your appearance.

Don't let arthritis destroy your self-image. Watch your weight. Keep yourself clean and neat.

Learn everything you can about arthritis.
You will feel more in control if you know about your disease. You may discover information that can help you. The Arthritis Foundation can supply you with educational material.

Join a support group.
Local chapters of the Arthritis Foundation offer support groups for teens with arthritis. Many hospitals have programs for teens with arthritis as well. Teens in support groups discuss common school, family, and social problems and share solutions.

Ask for help if you need it.
Everyone needs help from time to time. In turn, you can find some way to help others. For example, you might learn to be a good listener. Everyone needs someone who will listen to concerns and worries.

Get counseling if you need it.
It is normal to feel angry and depressed from time to time. If these feelings don't go away, talk with someone who can help. This person might be a school counselor, a support group member, or a mental health counselor.

Put your illness in its place.

Try not to let juvenile rheumatoid arthritis be the focus of your life. Focus on your abilities and not your disabilities. Develop interests and hobbies. Do volunteer work. Get out and enjoy yourself. Involve yourself with friends as much as possible.

Meg thinks of herself as an average 13-year-old. She thinks she has a good life, **Meg, Age 13** except for one roadblock. She has juvenile rheumatoid arthritis. Her disease was diagnosed when she was 18 months old. She's had a lot of practice learning to live with the disease. Meg says she doesn't let the pain get the best of her.

Meg enjoys swimming. In fact, she's on her school's swim team. Meg also likes to ride her bike, play the piano, and roller skate. She even has a paper route. Her disease sometimes gets in the way of delivering papers. When she has a flare, her mom and brother help her out. Meg has this to say: "All you kids with juvenile rheumatoid arthritis, get off your bottoms and enjoy life. After all, you only have one life to live!"

Juvenile Arthritis

Points to Consider

A teen who uses a wheelchair or crutches might have trouble moving around in a typical house. What could family members do to make their home more accessible?

If you had a friend with juvenile rheumatoid arthritis, how might that affect your life?

Do you know anyone who has a chronic illness? How does that person cope? How does the person's family cope?

Chapter Overview

Researchers are finding new ways to treat rheumatoid arthritis and are developing more effective drugs. Better methods for replacing joints are being developed. Research is also under way to find a cure for juvenile rheumatoid arthritis.

Many doctors now take a more aggressive approach to treating juvenile rheumatoid arthritis.

Stress management has become an important part of treating arthritis. Learning to relax can ease pain.

Teens with juvenile rheumatoid arthritis can take charge of their pain. They can be in control of their arthritis.

Chapter 7

Looking Ahead

Teens with juvenile rheumatoid arthritis may worry about the future. They wonder what will happen to them and to their disease. It might go away. It might get worse. They have no way of knowing. Teens with juvenile rheumatoid arthritis can have hope, however. Scientists and doctors continue to search for better ways to treat the disease. They may even find a cure.

Searching for a Cure

The search for a cure focuses on genes. Genes control characteristics that are passed from parents to children. Eye color and hair color are examples of inherited characteristics.

Today children can be vaccinated against measles, smallpox, and polio. The vaccine keeps children from getting the disease. Experts predict that a vaccine against rheumatoid arthritis will be available someday.

Scientists believe that some children and teens inherit a tendency toward juvenile rheumatoid arthritis. Something in the child's or teen's body or environment triggers the immune system to attack the joints. Researchers hope to identify this unknown factor. Then they can develop a way to defend against it.

Researchers also hope to develop a test for juvenile rheumatoid arthritis. Doctors could use the test to identify children at risk for juvenile rheumatoid arthritis. Treatment could begin before symptoms develop.

New Approach to Drug Therapy

Treatment for juvenile rheumatoid arthritis usually begins with weaker drugs. This approach is changing. Research suggests that the most serious joint damage occurs in the early stages of juvenile rheumatoid arthritis. As a result, many doctors now believe that treatment should begin with stronger drugs.

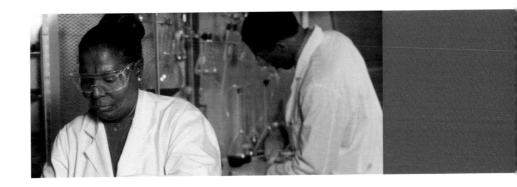

An anticancer drug called methotrexate has become more important in treating juvenile rheumatoid arthritis. The drug has been used to treat adult rheumatoid arthritis and childhood cancer for 30 years. It appears to be safe. The long-term effects of methotrexate on young patients, however, are not entirely known.

New Drugs

Scientists are always experimenting with new drugs to treat juvenile rheumatoid arthritis. They are working on better anti-inflammatory drugs to relieve pain. They also are working on drugs that will interrupt only the immune system's attack on the joints. Scientists hope to find drugs that will not interrupt the whole immune system. Scientists also hope to discover drugs that will be effective without troublesome side effects.

Leila and Renie are best friends. The girls

Leila and Renie, Ages 14 and 15

met in a support group for teens with juvenile rheumatoid arthritis. Their support group leader told them about an experimental drug for juvenile rheumatoid arthritis. Researchers were looking for children and teens to test the new drug. Leila and Renie qualified for the study. They both had arthritis in five or more joints. Both had been treated unsuccessfully with methotrexate.

Leila and Renie agreed to be in the study. They received injections of the new drug for four months. After the trial period, Leila's symptoms had almost disappeared. The only side effect was a mild cough. Renie showed no improvement. She still felt stiff and sore.

Juvenile Arthritis

Today people with kidney disease can undergo kidney dialysis. The dialysis machine cleans the poisons out of the blood. A similar device is being developed for people with rheumatoid arthritis. The machine filters arthritis-producing substances from the blood.

Methods for Coping With Pain

Drug therapy and exercise have been the main treatments for juvenile rheumatoid arthritis and other forms of arthritis. Doctors and therapists now recognize the role stress plays in arthritis. Stress can make muscles tight and tense. It can add to arthritis pain. Stress management also is becoming an important part of treatment programs.

People with arthritis can use several methods to help them relax. One method is biofeedback. Biofeedback uses a machine to teach people how to control their muscles. Another method is yoga. Yoga combines gentle exercise and special breathing techniques. Relaxation tapes help many people fall asleep at night.

Looking Ahead

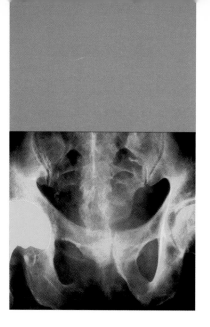

Improvements in Joint Surgery

Arthritis severely damaged Jamar's joints. At age 14, he had surgery to replace his hip joints. The next year doctors replaced his knee joints. Jamar is glad he had the surgery. The artificial joints make it easier for him to get around.

Jamar, Age 15

People with artificial joints eventually need to have them replaced. Artificial joints wear out. Jamar may need to have surgery again in 10 or 15 years. Scientists are working on new kinds of artificial joints. By the time Jamar needs surgery again, artificial joints will last longer. It will be easier to replace hip and knee joints, as well as other joints.

Looking Ahead

Current research on rheumatoid arthritis is exciting. It promises better ways of treating this painful condition. Teens with juvenile rheumatoid arthritis do not have to wait. They can take charge of their arthritis now. They can manage their pain. In the process, they will not only feel better but also develop coping skills. They can become more mature, thoughtful individuals.

Points to Consider

If you had juvenile rheumatoid arthritis, would you volunteer to test a new drug? Why or why not?

Do you know anyone who has had a hip or knee replaced? How did the surgery help the person?

What can you do to help promote awareness of juvenile rheumatoid arthritis?

What can you do to keep your own joints healthy?

Glossary

cartilage (KAR-tuh-lij)—soft tissue found in the joints; cartilage keeps bones from rubbing together.

chronic (KRON-ik)—continuing for a long time; a person with a chronic disease or illness may have it throughout life.

contagious (kuhn-TAY-juhss)—capable of being spread from person to person

contracture (kuhn-TRAK-chur)—a joint that becomes bent in a fixed position

fatal (FAY-tuhl)—capable of causing death

flare (FLAIR)—a period of increased disease activity

immune system (i-MYOON SISS-tuhm)—the system that protects the body from illness and disease

inflammation (in-fluh-MAY-shuhn)—redness, swelling, heat, and pain

ophthalmologist (ahf-thuhl-MAH-luh-jist)—an eye doctor; an ophthalmologist can perform surgery on the eyes.

pauciarticular (paw-suh-ar-TIK-yuh-luhr)—a type of juvenile rheumatoid arthritis that affects four or fewer joints

polyarticular (pah-lee-ar-TIK-yuh-luhr)—a type of juvenile rheumatoid arthritis that affects five or more joints

remission (ri-MISH-uhn)—a period when there are no active signs of the disease

rheumatoid (ROO-muh-toid)—a common type of arthritis in which the joints become inflamed

rheumatologist (roo-muh-TAH-luh-jist)—a doctor who specializes in all kinds of arthritis

systemic (siss-TEM-ik)—a type of juvenile rheumatoid arthritis that affects the whole body; affecting the whole body.

For More Information

Aaseng, Nathan. *Autoimmune Diseases*. New York: Franklin Watts, 1995.

Aldape, Virginia. *Nicole's Story: A Book About a Girl With Juvenile Rheumatoid Arthritis*. Minneapolis: Lerner, 1996.

Gold, Susan Dudley, and Brian J. Keroack. *Health Watch: Arthritis*. Parsippany, NJ: Crestwood House, 1997.

Huegel, Kelly. *Young People and Chronic Illness*. Minneapolis: Free Spirit, 1998.

LeVert, Suzanne. *Teens Face to Face With Chronic Illness*. New York: Julian Messner, 1993.

Useful Addresses and Internet Sites

The Arthritis Foundation and
The American Juvenile Arthritis Organization
1330 West Peachtree Street
Atlanta, GA 30309
1-800-283-7800

Arthritis Society of Canada
393 University Avenue, Suite 1700
Toronto, ON M5G 1E6
CANADA
1-800-321-1433 (in Canada)

National Arthritis and Musculoskeletal and
Skin Diseases Information Clearinghouse
National Institutes of Health
1 AMS Circle
Bethesda, MD 20892-3675

Pediatric Rheumatology
The Hospital for Special Surgery
535 East 70th Street
New York, NY 10021

Arthritis Canada
http://www.arthritis.ca
Provides education about many types
of arthritis

National Institute of Arthritis and
Musculoskeletal and Skin Diseases
http://www.nih.gov/niams/
Provides information on the causes, treatment,
and prevention of arthritis

The Arthritis Foundation
http://www.arthritis.org
Offers information on arthritis, includes
surveys, and provides links to other sites

The American Juvenile Arthritis Organization
http://www.arthritis.org/ajao/
Provides information on the types of
juvenile arthritis